Leonard Schwartz
Words Before the Articulate

by Leonard Schwartz

Objects Of Thought, Attempts At Speech

Exiles:Ends

Gnostic Blessing

Words Before the Articulate

Words Before
the Articulate

New and Selected Poems

Leonard Schwartz

Talisman House, Publishers
Jersey City, New Jersey

Published by Talisman House, Publishers
129 Wayne Street
Jersey City, New Jersey 07302

Some of these poems first appeared in: *Agni, Alea, American Letters and Commentary, Asylum, Central Park, Denver Quarterly, First Intensity, Five Fingers Review, Frank, The Literary Review, Pearl, Poetry New York, Talisman, Trafika*, and *The World*. The poem "Meditation" appeared as a Cloud Press chapbook.

Library of Congress Cataloging-in-Publication Data

Schwartz, Leonard, 1963-
    Words before the articulate : new and selected poems / Leonard
Schwartz.
        p.   cm.
    ISBN 1-883689-54-6 (cloth : alk. paper). -- ISBN 1-883689-53-8
(pbk. : alk. paper)
    I. Title.
PS3569.C5665W67   1997
811'.54--dc21   97-10827
                                                                    CIP

For Mingxia

Contents

V. New Poems

Words Before the Articulate

I. *from* Objects Of Thought, Attempts At Speech

Dictionary

Yesterday the dictionary scattered, fell like leaves.

Not a scattering universally attended,
nor the eclipse of scattered truths, nor
        a human scattering, of human seed.

It was a scattering of all the words that did not catch—
        and none of them did—
a fallow fantasia of language, meaning less
than any of the points of light in a planetarium

until finally, almost unbearably,
this scattering became the world at large.

As You Run Up The Stairs

"I seized it and opened it, and in silence I read the first passage on which my eyes fell." —St. Augustine, *The Confessions.*

Story of a garden:
in the middle of the story,
an account of the will.
Mysterious process: twisting
and turning in bronze-silver chains.
Golden reproaches, opening a book,
where the random eye falls.
The shaping of thought a difficult work,
never completed, or never begun.
Searching in thought for what you were thinking:
whirling to look when nothing is there.

Flesh, color, speech:
these exist by the rivalry
amongst little phrases.
The struggle to conceive,
sounds that palpitate and style the possible:
distant horizons that complicate a ghetto
in a grove, in the shadow of a city
that goes on writing.
Enclosing circles:
it pained and they gave me something
to quell the pain.
Searching in books for what's to be said:
whirling in thought as you run up the stairs.

The space of the mind
in constant retreat from space,
the voices we hear,
no longer coming from things.
A glance at the floor:
no rational argument can ever succeed
in calming such doubts. Yet no one
can wield these words, without adding
phantasms to the real. *The language supports the facsimile*,
ideality leaps in the hands.
Searching in thought for a way to get out:
it pained and they gave me something
to quell the pain.
Enclosing circles: twisting
and turning in bronze-silver chains.
Whirling to leave when no way is there.

Between Perception

The objects now offered
were beyond any wearying:
a small coffee, whose caffeine flick
adds to the real. The phoenix,
the moment when the phoenix
rises from the ashes.
An ambulance siren reddening the morning
Then the ambulance in ashes too:
afterglow of the phoenix torch
A silence as if of touch.

Irritation at the heart of things
what you meant by the poem suddenly at a distance
And the sun no longer visible
not so much due to the sky—
Suddenly the poem at such a great distance—
as to the mind's turning away.

Despairing of the real.
Kids on the street,
burning potato chips:
my thinking at first it was a bird.
A moment of fright as the shriveled embers
struggle to flutter away.
Angry rush of air:
breath of the spirit into a walk without words.
In the mind that which suffocates
comes to nourish. That which is beyond thought

becomes a kind of bread.
The soul on fire: the illusion of souls.
     But the fire, real.
"Am I invisible?", a man in a rag
challenges from the corner, begging for change.
Abrupt, what we see, what we don't,
its movement past, and always beyond.
My thought in my mouth
but thought out of breath.
Yes, yes, you *are* invisible
as everything real is made invisible
in the economy of need.

✻

Awakening from some exhausting depth
to the proximity of the eye-lash
and a tentative perception of light.
Sweet, this sweat, desire yet combing
          the reaches of the body.
Her body asleep next to yours:
the fire, and the consciousness that survives it.
Mornings in such sleep, rapture dissolved,
stripped of identities, such as they were.
A cross-section of lust suddenly exposed to itself
as sated and done, yet desire still humming.
Life in the bed, eliding the facts.
Watching her sleep; others' awakenings.

✻

The way the least visited museum
creaks when you enter. A long trip
for nothing, going two ways.
Stupor mundi : the faces in the subway.
Though the city sometimes arches its back,
blazes even, in the oblivion of its rebirth.
Then the distant veins tremble
as they circulate the living,
always the living, slowly towards their dens.
The city: a museum of unheard of contents.
Where handling the specimens is allowed
except that they handle you and you are one of them.
Excessive, the touching that goes on in this
imponderable vault. You lose yourself there.
You reel beneath the sheets as it roars under.
Stupor returns but in the form of joy.

Cemetery in the sun.
Before, only birds.
Then we come before the open grave:
she openly, uncontrollably, shakes.
Oh God, they're putting him into the ground.
Incredulous fact of her dead son,
hit by a truck in Galilee.
Maybe there's some mistake, I want to see his face,
she's cried. The face left unrecognizable,
	they'd examined his hand.
Oh God, they're putting him into the ground.
It closes you off, the cemetery gate,
leaves you alone in a world of mourning
over which the sun plays as if mourning were

an ordinary thing. Docile rows of polished cars,
an anguish running through the flesh:
the whiteness of the stones in a place
where others of your family have already been buried.
Yet a kind of indifference settles in
as if all this could be avoided by defiance
or good taste. Wondering about emotion,
how it vanishes only to then grab you by the chest.
His body, flown all the way back to Long Island,
        just for this ritual.
The sun filters through the hair of those erect.
The grass, green, and the breeze, softly blowing.
Sea gulls: the proximity of the sea.
A silence as if of touch.

Desire

"How should we ever go on except for desire,
or more, except that desire were disproportionate
to its means, its object, and, at last, to anything here?"
                                        —William Bronk

The Coursing

Sorrows, cloistered in the soul.
Pouring out of offices, crowds of souls in pain,
their lurch and thrash in the nets of becoming.
An inquisitrix of light arcs down the sidewalk,
stabbing the scene with pleasure, lashing up the avenue.
Caught in an exquisite misstep, illusion
and its necessity, Necessity's indifferent coursing,
the fountain and the contents of the fountain,
their pink indifferent foaming.
"How should we ever go on except for desire,
or more, except that desire were disproportionate
to its means, its object, and, at last, to anything here?"

Opening

Orifice where the light forges itself:
soft "V", from which I'm never coming out.
Her naked lips pressed back, what transfixes
her sex, the lapping of my tongue. Irony withers
when all is wet, what flows from its collapse:
giddiness of affirmation free from Babel
the glow there like the glowing of the excited silver moon
the words regaining their hunger for the infinite.
All else only imagination's bender after hours,
aspiration giving way to rhetorical response.

Bound within desire's run, the sensation
of "no": and now, of "yes".
Closer to the center the tires screech.
Written naked in its road a cage that stands in space.
As with this glossy fountain, gleaming in the sun.
Where the heart had its accident, will again.
What ends in joy ends before joy's begun.

Beauty

It begins with sight, advances outward.
Delicate ocean water, mermaids on the waves.
What is fluid in her motions, in the fluid of her come.
Or the movement of a weeping willow
where another rhythm rules: the pond
where the city masquerades as nature. A voice
among the voices to which the voice responds.
Solitude expressing itself in an expressive overflow.
Lust, for control, sucking, to be comforted.
What gleams of desire, and what hisses
of desire. *The cache of the crotch.*
Where words would flag in the absence of first flesh,
an alphabet of pubic curls. Beautiful,
the way she glows, when I call her beautiful.
To say her name would be to name her.
Except she makes me pass from what
would limit to repose in what she is.
In what is not: a single coursing of the soul.
A heightened sense that time and desire
can coincide, indeed. Pressing against
her breasts away from time.
Already rushing away, that sense,
as quickly as will the light.

✺

The most fantastic movement of the mind
is self-forgetfulness, still rich with thought:
in a nutshell, tenderness. These are the hands
that carry out the text at hand.
With its marvelous, its private
Sensitivities, the sexual fruit responds.

꒛

Reawakening

An emotion that speaks in buoyant gold.
How the body awakens to its vaster vision.
Graceful movements, as with a flipper:
some great half-fish of feeling
undulating in the light-filled morning.
Nothing moves. A comb lies on a wicker trunk.
Reality is what you look for here, not dreams' debris.
As if the clarity of the features of the woman's face
should stamp the room as well. Always delight before
darkness, or darkness before delight, or maybe not,
this unpredictability causing you a rapturous suspense.
It begins in sight, the green waves
lapping at your sides. A feeling
that fixes you with a transfixing look.
Deep blue eyes in a sonorous key.
A map of Central Park, a room
that sways in pine. Plenitude of things,
their sources elsewhere. The sensation of reflection,
sudden presencing of what was unseen before.
With that, a new measure. Electrical things
all turned off, but thought electric.
Each particular, aroused.
And no prohibitions.

Meditation

God and all his simulacra
were part of our physiology,

part of the rapture of meditation
whose whalebrow lies lustrous here,

the protuberance of Manhattan reascending
into sight as if by sway of light;

we are t-shirts, boots, forelocks,
the besouled custodians

of a dark-skinned skyscraper
equivalent to the night.

Not the beached and denuded sea-beast,
nor a species bound for extinction;

Not a monster with a heart
but the heart, that monster;

Not everything is appointed
and it is good that this island was not appointed

Yet still arrives,
the exactitude of form

In the water,
the grandeur of the unseen beneath.

To be swallowed up
by a city's invisible contingencies,

The specifically contingent ecstasy of
the city as the island as the fish,

A spawning awareness of something
larger than one's own decline:

Yet this ecstatic equation—the denizen
as Jonah as escapee but only from himself—

Is not intelligible to the escapee denizen,
and the custodianship of the contingent

Remains unfelt. God and all his simulacra
lead us to bed. Necessity is still sought.

An impenetrable self-reference
locks the only door.

The city too resubmerges . . .
it is as if with God's cooling

All that which suffered the creation
were now speaking the first words of nothingness,

An invisible parlance of visible things
sealing the obscurity of the spoken

Within the obscurity of each skin—
as if the half-lit buildings of this zone

In their interiors encircled only
eyeless nomads impassioning each other,

Simulacrum realizing itself,
struggling together, absolute in tenderness.

2

In the face of God's repose,
God was inflamed:
that was the God of both
repose and flame.
A God that for the first time
glimpsed itself, but mistook
itself for another (what other
would God imagine himself to be?)
Or, dimly conscious of its error,
the divine denial of a God
unwilling to see itself
as the source of an
elegance of words
but a world in ruins.

What is, cannot be,
cries out to be burned away.
God is what cries out,
and the anger that falls upon that cry.
Sky raging at the sky
in lightening strokes:
self-flagellating spirit,
sparked by the eye
to strike at itself.

Like what happens

at the limits of the self
at the moment we choose
not to recognize them.

Like boundaries of body,
categories of thought,
confounded by speech,
the lovers lie entwined
at the heart of God's lash.

Pause: even patience
is delirium, or else we would not
conceive of each hour as *waiting*.
As waiting for the next God.

3

The vision of the eye impaired
not by its own deficiency
or by any real obstacle
but by a deficiency in what *can* be seen.

This is the further storm.

The death not of the subject
but of the object.

The world beyond
out to lunch.

    Static yet supple tree
ecstatic in the sun:
reality and its report.
The rushing loins of light

As if a proof of life.

Misleading headline:
the motorcade of the imagination
brought all traffic to a stop.
I was there, and I can say:
nothing in that stream abated.

Yet until the voice
        makes the separation
a testament to beauty
        and a misleading headline read as one—

The voice not of God
    but of whoever it is
found lying amid the rubble
    not far from the tree,

A voice that does not say a thing
    but whose mythical presence
shapes the difference,
    grounds each word.

Your own voice.

Your own silence.

Amid the rubble of good and evil.

4

On certain mornings it brings no joy to imagine the stringy, golden light of afternoon. As if to look to the sun were to realize that the sun is a vestige: the shadow thrown off by a sculpture is more the light of man.

At work in the hand, then, the generative activity behind everything visible.

Myth, myth remaking noon: the sculpture is free, we are moulded. Marble becomes flesh, we become stone. *The struggle of the physical bodies to define themselves out of the stone within which they are still held bound.* Those bodies, toiling desperately, desperation in their eyes. The half-lit towers immobile on the shore.

It happens too that sculpture comes back to grapple with our unpolished hands. Like us it wants to be the Other; in being made, desire flowed from us to it, until it is what we desire, until it desires. Of course it desires: it is our creation, made in our image. And almost as we might have dreamt it, the sculpture rushes towards us. We look up at it, catch at it with whatever tricks of matter lie at hand.

The city is such a stunt, made from thought though sculpted in thoughtlessness. The whirl of a weather helicopter, the clawfoot of a building, the hammering in the street as the street is hammered out: when to such movements we awake, we awake *within the very object that we seek.*

Not to the effigy in the mirror, charred black from fire and deja vu. Not as a point of light without a form, a fear upon the pillow on the bed.

But as participants in its being.

16

5

Before sorrow
it came
to fire summer

Before seasons
it *was* fire

Without it
a sleep as deep
as total eclipse.

A rapture of meditation
no longer
recognizable in the light of day:

Plunge, bravely, then, into each day's generation.

II. *from* Exiles: Ends

Form

An immediacy of mind,
a chaos built of stones;
a foyer, of astonishing brilliance.

And a limousine, pulling out of the familiar.

I belonged to the far off parapet
                    and was part of it
part of the cage of fire on the limo's dashboard.

An instant, a movement,
a nerve that doesn't stand a chance

to order the chaos yet leave the astonishment blaze.

Exiles: Ends

It adds itself to the list of other places
as if a hand leaving its signature upon the earth—

    A place
among the other places
that situates the rest.
An avenue of sounds multiplied
five-thousand times.
Walking for blocks,
the heart growing hoarse.
Facetious facial twitch,
an exposed woman's shoulder,
an exposed white strap.

Given the facts of solitude and of death,
what can matter more than a despair
capable of suddenly flaming into rapture?

Walking out of the way to buy
the milk of my mother back.
Other wants, tugging away.
Running out of time on this earth,
always, always.
The illusion of permanence
a permanent illusion.
The partial vision of the living.
All projects of the word,
illusions of the word.
Welfare hotels, construction teams:
a dried-up scale
falling from the eye.
It should and it shouldn't
happen this way, and it does.

Fumes of our loudest fears,
skull seared by the pressing heat:
fruit markets, funeral homes.

Thinking nothing, walking for blocks.
Central Park West, Columbus Avenue,
the sun a kind of windfall profit
trickling down. Thought is inseparable
from my nature, thought Descartes:
it really is a saving grace,
the sun, an object above
sustaining the shadows below.
When did things grow so solid?
At the joust: sensation's lance
shattered on a shield,
leaving only finite perception,
perceiver and perceived,
the writer, the reader,
in uneasy complicity.

And the loser is feeling, always feeling.
Erasing sadness and too extreme joy.
Adding and subtracting parts of a book.
Revising, revisiting, reforming the past.
Resume-writing, writers of "ought".
Looking at a duck in the pond in the park,
panicking, then lurching away.
Drinking coffee like a duck eats bread.
Caffeine in the aquarium's tanks
unnerving the fish. Empty stomach
eating itself. Feeding my frenzy.
Falling in Canada, acid rains freeze.

The music contains desire
in negative form. Condensation

of love into despair.
She waited at the train-station,
glowing with warmth.
Arrival at night, laughter at first:
then frantic illusions, lingering cares,
three-dimensional flesh, caressing her hair.
Desire as such, rapture at odds.
Love-making bodies, baking like bread.
Entwining intent, bodies at rest:
saddening hold and light of slow ferment.
The cynical self, fermenting
inside the foment of lives.
Discord of pleasure,
hand on her thighs.

Cast-iron cots in the soup kitchen/shelters.
"Almost like India by now", he added, "the sheer
 number of them, all begging for change":
editor of a Marxist journal who knows only Newport,
issue on Latin America coming out next.
The hemorrhage of another scream.
the impossible questions the homeless are posed.
Human brows crashing against the stone,
newspaper account: the cardboard is comfortable.
Cities' center, the eye of the exile.
A whole fever of rednesses,
one disfigured sky. The word: a lie
that never tires, that reads till the end.

Rage on the sleeves, but the sleeves never real.
Tripping on truth, retying one's shoes,
stooping to use tools one's never thought useful.
Meeting someone new, thirty years my elder
who as I undress demands to be called "mother".
The frenzy for Freud. The disappointment,

Exiles: Ends

her's: nothing forthcoming. Brief spoken words,
hasty departures, though the idea appeals
for a brief sparkling instant in another man's brain.

Swirl of identity, nothing the same.
Invalid experience, frantic tries elsewhere.
Cars in the dark, driving or parked,
hoods glistening with rain.
The light that passes
with the passing of an hour.
The light a day contained.
Each instant counts, each instant counting.
Self-from-which-all-poetry-stems.
Insisting on the impersonal "who" that I am.
Sleek streets of night,
streets cobbled with bone.
Facing the wall, eyeing the phone:
cement in the thighs, exhaustion as such.

Memory of other cities, ducks resting
silently on East Berlin waters.
Soot of the war still on the streets.
Elegiac feeling in the aftermath
of nightfall, elation of discovery:
Kristallnacht temple, crystal clear night.
Exciting source, this fallen synagogue,
covered with boards, exodus still-born.
Returning to the ruin, again and again,
booking the gloom in memory,
promising it more time, shivering cold.
Dry lactate of stars, suckle of sorrow,
blistering loneliness crouched in the stone.
Night — exile — elixir — exodus —
Seizing the heart, nothingness foaming.

Tender Dissection:

On Bogden Borkowski's *Le Poeme*

(*Le Poeme* is a twelve-minute movie made in 1985 by Bogden
Borkowski. The step-by-step filming of the dissection of a
human corpse, *Le Poeme*'s sound-track consists of an impas-
sioned reading of Arthur Rimbaud's great poem, "The
Drunken Boat".)

"To remember suddenly that you have a skull— and not lose
your mind over it!"

—E.M. Cioran

Autopsied before our eyes, this corpse rebels: we can hear it in
our ears. It then becomes a question of how much trust we can put in
the word as spoken. As Marc Guillaume points out in "The Metamor-
phosis of Epidemia", the word, in its normal usage, is a virus passed
from person to person, exchanged by personal contact, until finally,
infecting a group of persons, it produces ideological changes and
behavioral symptoms.

But what can be said when the word in question has its origins in
the utterances of a corpse; do corpses carry viruses? The body in its
most concrete sense—stripped not only of thought but desire, not
only of its life but its flesh, gently and even tenderly dragged towards
a Nothingness beyond Nothingness: this body at the terminus point
before vanishing in favor of a bag of organs, digits, and bones—a rib
cage, an eye, a leg, vocal chords, a brain; this body, which is silenced
only once it is zipped up inside its body bag; this body, turned inside
out, turns out to be the site of the word, and not just of any old
words, but those of the "Drunken Boat".

Who or what is it that rebels when the poem is uttered at the final
moments before the body ceases? What is the outer limit, the ex-
treme outpost, of this body's sense? "The body's sense": what then is

this body? Perhaps Borkowski means only to contribute his two cents to the debate surrounding Rimbaud himself? Arthur, you will recall, may have confessed and converted on his death-bed, and in any case was under intense pressure to do so from his sister. So that here, perhaps, this cadaver, surrogate for Rimbaud, recants any confession he may have given under duress, by treating us in his post-mortem state to an impassioned reading of the crowning achievement of his bad-boy career. Released from the suffocating presence of his sister, Rimbaud cancels his confession, and admits instead that he is still tempest-tossed. Incidentally, they say that Rimbaud's legendarily difficult mother would later dig up the remains of Rimbaud's body, as well as the body of his other sister, in order to rebury them both on a new family plot, complete with a grotesque monument in the worst bourgeois taste. The mother, finding that the sister's coffin had been eaten apart and its contents spilled, was nonetheless able to salvage her daughter's teeth and hair, which she calmly gathered up in her arms and carried away. No doubt if Arthur's post-mortem state had remained such a vocal one as that of *Le Poeme*, she would have been as equally deaf to his unrecalcitrant cry.

But no, this cadaver is not simply an attempt to revive or take sides in the old Rimbaud debates. Instead it is, deposited on a spool of film, a contribution to the ontology of poetry, a disgorging of light. Rimbaud's poem suffuses the screen; the word is an image. This suffusion—poetry—is also the body's violence, the last moment of the body as sense and form, before being forcibly returned to brute unformed matter.

When a part of the body is removed, it enters the aesthetic realm. The living organism is transformed, through such dissection, into a non-living but beautiful object, as static as it is partial. The painter plucks out his eye in order to contemplate it. This dissection, however, is of a different order. There is no longer any central living organism with which the severed parts may be contrasted, as all is here in dismemberment and flux; there is no longer any whole to which a part can be traced, at least by the time the body is finally zipped up inside the body bag at the end. The distinctions between whole and part, and living and dead, are thus superseded. As the eyes are unzipped from their sockets, the rib cage undone from its cavity, the "I" is paralyzed. Simultaneously, we realize two things: our horror at having a body to which all this can happen; and underneath that, the blue light, the consciousness of what it is to have the body that we do: this stuff in movement, our visceral awareness of this beating and pulsing whole. "Bone", "blood", "fat", are in fact words that are too abstract to describe this body, as are "lips", "eyes", and "chest"; all these words have nothing to do with the fleeting sensation of the body as body, this capacity for movement and presence. Pessimists might insist that the body's gesture and presence, and the feeling of horror before the body's existence, are actually one and the same awareness, as if from some deeper perspective presence and gesture were ruled by that horror. But I am uncertain. True, to be conscious of the body as body is to understand the fatality of its situation, the inconsequential speck of time which constitutes its history. All the same, I am conscious of my body now; strangely, this body is more palpable than those pessimists. And the truth is that this body, though of course the most anti-representational of stuff on the one hand, is all the same still an image, and an image, against all logic, is something heard; the image is in the word: what is heard, "The Drunken Boat", stream of absolute rebellion.

Indeed, the knife does peel away layer after layer of emotion, until finally we realize that dissection is the inverse of love-making. When the knife cuts into the corpse, the dead body gives way and surrenders up pieces of itself, until it is nothing. But when one living body gently cuts across another living body in love-making, or when the word, tenderly uttered, issues forth in a consciousness of the other's body, an image of the other's hand, the other's hair and eyes, there is a surrender of another kind. In love, the living surrenders itself wholly to presence, a surrender it wholly survives, even as its awareness is taken apart and rebuilt as passion; while this corpse, taken apart at its roots—this chest, that once sweated in love, these lips, stripped from their everyday position - is also overcome by a singular passion, the passion of its rebellion against the mechanical and mineral disintegration of its being. The living body, sweating in love, is overcome by ecstasy, which is to say that in the embrace there is a complete absorption, a disappearance into the others living form; here there is a surrender to the knife. The love-making body plunges into its counterpart and wraps it up, keeps it warm, entangles itself there, vanishing as a particular entity, while the carver's hands plunge coldly into the dissected body, transforming it into matter. What these bodies have in common is that they are both pressed to the extreme limits, of matter on the one hand and poetry on the other. In "Le Poeme", these two limits overlap; the dissection itself is never violent; only the cadaver's reaction is, and even then, there is an aura of tenderness that presides over the whole affair. So what if a piece of wood discovers it's a violin, so what if a violin discovers it's a piece of wood! In both instances, the body is an other. If the orgasm is a paroxysm that lasts an instant, and despair a paroxysm that lasts a lifetime, then the poem is the general name for the paroxysm that lasts till the final instants before physical decomposition.

Remove the sack of muscle that covers the heart, remove the heart itself; this voice continues. Remove the esophagus, the voice-box, the brain; this voice continues. The poem too is pressed between the pages of an anthology someplace, a dead text; the poem too lies there, quiet, entombed, unread. The cadaver is the site of a drunken passion. The body is an other. The image is something heard. The image is in the word.

By passionately throwing myself at my condition, I found myself tenderly embracing my sleep; by embracing my fears I lived my nightmares. Daily reality holds to its line of reasoning; but when I felt the blade fall, I knew I'd been cut loose from even the worst of these.

We can easily imagine the cadaver muttering something like this by way of an apology for not having had time to throw something on before inviting us in.

The chaotic visage of this cadaver can of course be charted into a larger scheme: of many other bodies: of buildings and bodies: of minds and bodies, and so on. Alternatively, the body might be thought of, as in the old Kojevian vision of the Other, as the passive matter I strain to master but instead am enslaved by. Alexandre Kojeve, you will recall, was the philosopher who introduced Hegel to the French, but in so doing, opted to concentrate on little more than the few chapters in *The Phenomenology of Spirit* that dealt with the master-slave relation. Influential teacher of Sartre, Merleau-Ponty, and others, Kojeve founded a whole tradition. The body was the master in that tradition; the mind, the slave, and at least in Hegel the slave, in his dialectical rebellion, wins. Insofar as it is inert and full the body initially overwhelms my empty and out of breath consciousness. Later the mind rebounds. But the game is fixed: from the Kojevian perspective (and that of its inheritors) there is no way of distinguishing one body from the other, all bodies being one mass of undifferentiated and heavy matter. No one body is sufficiently determinate to qualify itself as different from the others, as "this one" or "that one"; thus the body becomes an abstract Body.

The cadaver in question, however, is neither a dialectical loser nor an infinite regression; as I have indicated, it is as individualized as you or I. It flexes when we flex; there is no doubt about its authenticity. Perhaps, though, the demand to rise up above the body and subdue its immediacy, return its missing organs, dress it up and let it run down wider avenues, place it into a social context in order to trace its relations to other similar ones and to the epidemic of death that engulfs them all, is a less easy obligation to dismiss. After all, the drunken boat, lost among flotsam and weed, is related to a whole transcendental world of images and corpses, fish floating belly up, all manner of kelp, "dead men, pale and thoughtful, sometimes drifting by." I could foresee one day tracing the lines of force of this luminous underwater dialogue, or even the exact relation between my silence and your's. At present, however, I refuse to budge or hasten anywhere far from the prospecting of the pure body, of this body. So that the horror of life is also the drunkenness of art . . . in any case, the everyday is exploded by this feeling. And I saw in the violence of this emotion, my only chance at rebellion.

It's strange, I cannot even fully imagine what it would be to live without a leg. Yet I dare to try to imagine what it would be if my whole body were to be rendered as lifeless as something amputated. This corpse, the source of all my speech, the simulacra of a plenitude that's been destroyed.

Massacred, one organ after another stripped away, just as that picture of Western intellectual history has it that one belief after another has been torn from us by the roots and thus forever lost("God", "humanity", "the subject", etc.) so too this body, staring blindly, despite loss of mind, heart, vocal chords, continues talking. Listen! The absolute, the subject, consciousness, the body: why make of the body a victim of structure too?

III. *from* Gnostic Blessing

Gnostic Blessing I

for Peter Mittenthal

"Make yourself an ark of gopher wood; make rooms in the
ark, and cover it inside and out with pitch. Make a roof for
the ark, and finish it to a cubit above; and set the door of the
ark in its side; make it with lower, second, and third decks."
— The Lord to Noah, Genesis 6

Through successive swells he had—he had, the one who was not
Noah—only pretended to worship, not even aware, as God had
supposed, of the evils of the one world, the goodness of the other.
Now floods wound down their cold fingers over him, and he leapt up
to slash at the algae gathering in the very rain. That was about all he
and his family and his friends could do.

Later there were cross-beams in the raging sea, as impossible to
cling to as the sea itself, no matter how many times one tried—not
mirages of the drowning, but strips of a ghostly wood as real as the
water pouring from the fountains of the deep. This wood was a great
insult to human dignity.

But really, it was all a morbid dreambook, in which a being and a
deathless being fought together as over a terrible difference. No word
could ever permanently bind the notions of two such beings. Thus the
non-specialist grew insensible to everything but the possession of

rites, like a survey that begins to grow wearisome as the research drags on, leaving behind the uncanniness of pain for the security of becoming wooden faced, afloat, as the survivors had done in this case.

Now, it is still thundering, and this winter day is no exception, crowned not only by new forms of disease and distress but also by expansive regressions, both religious and rational, all marked by the phenomenon of trance and carried out in a wholly unlived way. But these tentatives will also sink, into one universal sump, surrounded by drowning sands, so that it will become a question simply of asking ourselves how we can examine the inner contents of our speech, trickling off as it usually does into hair-raising summaries of harassment, the body, with each new bulletin, wincing away from the megaphone of pain, and at the same time, preparing more of it. So that all that is left is the "I told you so" of the Pretenders, of the mad-farers, of those who were not saved from the flood, who piloted into the Darkness without a God to save them. Their's are the ghosts we "worship".

An Imaginary Rickshaw
for Heraclitus the Dark

Who is it that weeps
when it rains
your innermost thoughts

When the blades of an automatic editing
notch the grainy line
and the dreaming fractions rustle?

Perhaps this line will dissemble to infinity
but whoever you are
you are a creature that works by parts

By taking apart
by parting
or by attempting to dull the blade.

If all things turned into smoke,
the nostrils would still distinguish them.
Distinguish from one another then

These figurines of incense as they rise
lazily through the air
and then disappear from view

The enterprise of extension
not precisely becoming its opposite
but extending its enterprise into areas

Of unsuspected want and satiety
of near insubordination to matter
just as the living fibers yield up their sap

When stabbed,
and the smoke gently
strains against its smokiness.

❧

Everywhere Change and Stillness
indulge themselves
in shadowy interchange

And fall in love with hiding,
the purely auditory crossing over
into the perceptual

A carnal tradition
in which the body is reflected,
its interior simultaneity suspended in dimness

Too easily mistaken for a nominal chaos.
As if the choice of one thing bore witness
to a multiplicity of necessary contestations,

As if the record you were making for yourself
need never be edited
or taken apart for others eyes or ears.

Yet it cannot be denied
that Logos is more than ordinary law,
subtle yet discursive as it binds one to others

At once a logical statement
and faces absorbing heat from a flame,
a change in the fire, a sea that burns,

A storm cloud on the horizon.
By definition distant?
The shock of insight hits

And the personality is bridged,
recognition at the beginning of utterance
stripped and tender medium of wood.

So the wooden drums beaten on this the furthermost island
are islands of percussion when in your veins
or else the snapping of a twig outside

Or rafts departing from those islands
to the pounding of ritual drums
as for some ceremonial revel

For which the twigs are kindling.
Go ahead, pretend the "stuff"
with which you work is only stuff

Only continue to make of it
a late night bark
the sea worthiness of which cannot be known

Continue to break down matter
as it is handed over
speak in order to discover what to say.

꙳

To sleep in ash
but awaken aflame
part of the natural course

Of things,
where things are understood
as Logos.

No chance of turning down
this power of reasoning either
it would only come up again

And besides,
there is little evidence
of anything else to choose from.

Night-wanderers, Magians, Bacchanals,
Lenaeans, keepers of mystery . . .
knowing nothing of gods or heroes or what they are.

So then why deposit
your book in a temple
of Artemis

Why darken your language
to keep the commoners out
if ultimately everything must become

Everything else
and all the mysteries
transparent?

Blessed contradiction
philosopher of synthesis,
blessed contradiction.

So the Sibyl with raving mouth
uttering things mirthless,
unadorned, unsweetened,

Reaches with her voice
over a thousand years
because of the god in her.

Compared with this it is easy to comprehend
how the fire that burns the wood
is the wood

And how the water that swamps the bridge
can be conceived of as the bridge but none
of these niceties matter now only tell me Heraclitus

Who is it that is weeping
as we scatter and come together
approach and go away

What does this mirthless Sibyl know
how is it she can violate the laws of time
and of meaning

Who is pulling the rickshaw
next to which I feel myself to be
neither the servant nor the lord

But perhaps the very vehicle of their encounter
a flimsy chariot of planks or maybe rags
upon which everything else is riding?

Whose is the raving mouth
calling you forward into superstition
and dropping back behind your gaze?

Alexandria

Low in the marsh life sang its violent contrasts.
Fantastic, this song in the face of formlessness.
All of the participants had to muffle their own substance,
Scour themselves of mud. Low in the marsh
Life sang of an inner coherence to the crystalline sky,
Of an earth on which water or earth had never come to pass
Nor made of its failures gods it could not find.

By day, wild grasses, the solar fire displacing night,
By night, wild grasses, the sky's mineral vision.
But always all that was alive singing into formlessness
Until all the participants, whatever their form,
    suppressed what they were,
Becoming no more than incandescent pores,
Which, from another planet, might have been taken
    for clusters of paradise.

Monuments to the Not Yet Lived

The streets I walk down are an incorporating of English into proscriptions of disturbance, a rupturing of thought by contingency after contingency, an insurrection of the actual. The lamp in the shadow, the screen in the sky, a cave as the Real's source: all of these part of the simple plane over which one steps, intertwined in two places at once. Aftereffects of a dream sensation, apparitions in a sun shower, translating into vocal music, into a harmony of street noise where *street* means **event.** Verbalizing daylight, swelling as the phrases transfer across. Only so much has reinstated itself through my authorship during the course of one year that I can divine for you no more than a fictive awareness of any place I am. This is Siberia, the sleepwalkers after a long march through bitter cold and snow are reconnecting with their beds. William xyz was taken out of himself, if only to enter the underworld. I bend backwards like a bow to shoot forward towards all that I love, and that tautness is the future power of the past's repositories. And so on, down a finite number of invisible avenues spilling into the visible. So the well-nourished microcosm with its compliment of fillibrations shows itself willing to hazard a reasonable guess, and externalizes a soft and tattooed macrocosm at the distance of night. Over and over the future is reconfigured in this way, but the future too is finite and bears its freedom grudgingly.

On a point in technical procedure all the muses fall into vast disagreement, their voices demonstrating that wide-spread beliefs can combine into new kinds of complexes that sap the psyche because not believed first-hand evidence, only hearsay and intuition. Like a surgical operation in which the artificial organ is rejected, this way of thinking, although the organ is left in anyhow and *something* continues to function. Aren't we all suffocating for lack of some object capable of moving us out? The body is left without the tools to understand where its voices emanate from. Experiment finds itself in a new incarnation whose attributes cannot flourish. A friend says that it was a dialogue that sent all of those detachable souls onto the ice to die, and a dialogue that will bring them back, that we are already outside ourselves but that it is too lonely there to know it. Good and bad, then, that the bodily ailments retain everything. That the scanty trance-like mood that holds you down when you can do nothing finally erupts into vision. That a voice for thoughts relocates the wound. *One is always stopped just as one starts finding out where it is that the messages are written.*

How cruel that this wing with all its prison cells always seems to alter to meet the present's needs, that the psychological function makes the living pass through so much trouble, distorting even the derivation of that wing of cells. Imprisonment is more than a metaphor, it is a way of being. I always imagine myself next to something that is really very far away, feel myself perpetually on the approach, although it is for another time, the satisfaction, if at all. The awareness of confinement spills over into the allied acts of planning out a campaign of frustration and feeling the brunt of that planning in distanced form . . . So much is battle, the fields littered with dead mammals and burning skin, and all so that key messages might eventually experience interruption. The will is felt behind awareness, preparing its own demise in the wills of others . . . Out of a human consultation erupts a dreaded image of the fallen body, a derangement in nocturnal garb, a black language on colorless tablets, stones huddled around an inscription in rags. And all from impatience, from the fear of immobility, from the chafing of a confinement whose terms escape definition but whose culmination is a false relief that is only a further proof of the enormity of the exclusion that each being extends to each. In the end, it is euphoria that has been sabotaged.

Its strange that so much of who one is remains the same. Because there is pain in so much seeing. As hopes are ground down, ever more naive certitudes arise, their hovering routes connecting one perspective to the next. And just as a certain fragile mass of nebulae takes possession of the end of a lonely winter's day, and a mass of contingencies are the only thoughts, islets of desire gradually plait into monuments to the not yet lived. This is the time of day for a militant openness concerning spiritual acts, but this is also the time of day that refuses to open to anything. Refer us instead to some sort of law, to a procession of sanctions, to all sorts of deposit information that ought not to have been purchased—or even produced—in the first place. Pick up what one has been given, work it, better it, yes. But one can never be sure who's suitcase is who's. There is an effort made to keep track, but everything is so coextensive with everything else that one's bearings start to sag as under the weight of a drink, or as if we had uncovered an inexplicable weakness in our characters, the whole fractious nuclear jumble careening into view like a station wagon, the identity of space with the mind, and of the mind with its earliest memories, reducing us to the most passive of numerals, the numeral one. We **are** number one, always thought we were, always think we will be, however infantile it is to think so. Which explains why we cannot move, why at the heart of the cheer awaits a lengthening silence, a silence that can never be entered. And so the space we can move through becomes ever less.

The totality of the thought hurtles past, at the most filmy remove from the immediate. The eye is that film. Totality escapes it. We kill what we see.

As experience stands to reflection, so to the silence an absurd variety of upheavals. The more unlikely they are, the more passionate the trouble. Sometimes I fortify myself against them and retreat abroad, in a manner of speaking, simply dismissing the new realities by not being there, by releasing the mind's ethers. Or like those shreds of evidence some authors build into sweeping truths about life, no doubt as a matter of doing their job, I allow myself to inflate to fantastic proportions. Such declarations ache as they swallow reality, not exactly digesting all of it. This is a partial listing of how they ache: a partial listing too of how they deliver. Waiting for a phrase to open up to a series of phrases, and for a series of phrases to forget themselves as they become the actual. A question, then, of what value one assigns to that moment of forgetfulness. But I cannot stop to think now about any but the most immediate of truths, and those are that I have no mind, no body. *You must measure with your gaze the abolitions your gaze contains, point more explicitly to your quarrel with the world. You are an apprehension of all that is not and you must never withdraw from that, the sciences of the body more than willing to convert you to their object. Their's is a stern standpoint without contact with things themselves; they will always insist that you pay attention to their own awkward forms. But you will not. You will want to, mean to, but what you have forgotten will be stronger still, and nothing will be able to distract you from the act of futile recollection, no one will be able to prevent you from failing to remember all that is.*

The unsettledness of any strip of earth, investigators piercing beneath its bedrock, tracing a new line into all that tonnage. Returning to the surface, this interrogation makes contact with itself in an immediate nothingness of dark colors, listens, listens for an approximation of the total situation despite having just added something new, then lowers its head again, sinks its teeth down into the crust, like a thoughtful animal pawing into the vast body of a mineral wealth it cannot understand the purpose for. And although nothing here can be understood, the torso of the visible, the shifting truth, bring language to fulfillment. The nascent state misleads the dreamer, however long his history. A questionnaire half-filled out, comments half-abandoned to the others gaze, modulate into a less distant obscurity, restively extending itself over fundamental solidities that fade in turn. Slowly the exterior turns to look at itself as if it were some unkempt rustic type deposited abruptly in a vast metropolis. Spiny intersections overwhelm the eye, and mammoth spigots; even the tabletops inside a pancake house come informed by their own particular allure. Each street noise carries an imaginary rebuke, one to which one is more than willing to listen. These are the allures desired, the voices of imperative. They never last, but there are many sensitive points on the ear, some of which retain the memory in a form that at any moment can sing from the actual.

The shorthand must be disentangled from its expediency, the whole of perception calling to it. Offices rapidly closing down like lights on the mainland, until the whole Wall Street area resembles a ghost town, until you are alone at sea, the raw air on your face assuming the feel of necessity. Or taking a risk, wandering in Central Park well after nightfall, a strange white light glowing in the sky to the East Side. Do you know that in all my wanderings in Central Park after nightfall I have yet to meet a single soul? On the outskirts they walk their dogs, but at the heart of a thing there is nothing but what your eyes chance to see and your heart happens to feel. So much darkness goes by so quickly it is impossible to turn it into light. Then more walkers, more dogs. Taking a risk: the grounds are wet, the moisture will soon freeze. But to bring this over into language requires another turn in the obscurity, a further preparation of the grounds. Even at the heart of a thing there is nothing but what your eyes chance to see and your heart happens to feel, there is this total vacancy. The burly trees offer no assistance, slumbering in their metaphors. The lamps glow whitely, weakly, on the ragged fields. My love, you were confident and full of lofts, and from here, where you are not, where you appear to be invisible to yourself, I imagine I can see all of you. So many girders fly past, so much glass, it is impossible not to tremble from it, not to reel from the power of what is made. At the sight of such a creation, finite but extreme, the mind grows extreme, seeks the extremity of the finite, but finding nothing, stops. The extreme of beauty must be outside creation. Then more walkers, more dogs.

Everything that the people in a room have seen collects along a single line to which no one in the room has access. But outside that room the line appears a vertical figure.

Gnostic Blessing IV

Lines in Anticipation

I

The flesh is where the second life militates its bearings,
   insensible yet sensible,
As elation enacts its power, effortless prologue to the scythe.
So much of what is felt is lost along the way,
Is deepened in the recovery, is lost again,
The very nature of the porous to mislay its own interior,
   fall through its own sides.

A humidity, a moving weight in the windows
Reassembling the windows before my eyes.
From wholeness weaned—from whence the music?
   Pseudopods of a synonymous amoeba.
Alive in the silence of a body
   the ear develops the exact proportions of by hearing.

There is an opening to the second life here,
a find that unites the fissures of a world
   no longer obstacle.
A space between two times of day
   through which fires
a jet of water, carrying to term
the antipodes the flesh must break,
   not releasing.
As if to enter this tunnel of connected things
   was to overhear a community of desires
the very violence of which
   this language is the frank retention of.

The brain, a thing, is not a thing.
   No anthropos but
The torn anthropos that flutters
over the reaches of speaking,
   singular as a perforation.
The narrow space between my building and the next
a tear in human architecture, a perforation out.
"Hear, O _____ !" :
the body is its pre-objective bellowings,
   the whole of a nervous system tensing to listen.
Tensed night sky: the pupil of the animate eye:
   a letter descending in the form of a bird.
Envelope after envelope, at the latency of word.
All is addressed to the centrifuge of sensations
the mind now feels itself to be.

All must find itself in loss.

2

The necropoli arranged on the body,
the remains of ancestors memory
   can neither verify nor recall.

Waking world of skin. Cool rock of night.
Lifetimes triggered by an instant's fall
   suspected, unsuspected,
toppling through impermeability
downward (recollection)
downward (fall).

Afterwards a point of day filled with dark,
a bruise in memory oozing forth
    chivalrous profanations.
Nothing but the contingent here.
But nothing heard remains contingent long.
Within the language of philosophy
lies the language of archeology.
Archeologies of the possible
swelling into the music
    of a new elation.
Mnemosyne amongst her murmurings.
Lifetimes of reflection that someone
    might have stamped here, lost.

Open the door. Open the door
to the crypt. You will see who you are
    without your body.

                    3

An opening to the second life here
where the sun must be apprehended
    as powerfully enlarged.
Sunlight floods the city, sunlight runs the steps, sunlight
penetrates windowpanes, alleyways.
But it is the dark sunlight of the counter-sun,
    and nothing here is visible.

"Counter-sun ":
there is not yet any counter-apprehension.
First everything here would have to be reimagined, led back up
    from the matrical trace of the city
into the dazzling light of the counter-sun
    from fantasy to lucidity

---

led back into the dazzling life of the counter-sun
A condition which precedes its own embodiment
An original home prior to any garment
    this luminous emulsion of pre-natal nebulae
    this permeable figure of the imaginary-real
Light which appears dark but really is light
  the body as soil now blossoming, the human a humus
    for thinking and seeing without any eyes.

When that Sensation which must be   is,
matter ceases to do anything but breathe—
and the second life becomes the first.

Sight is one thing, light another.
And light has no need of sight
since nothing that stands within light itself
can be grasped by light.

The world demands explanation but is inexplicable.

4

We're our dying to attend to,
bend back the bow in dreams as we may
    elation peaks,
a syringe is driven into an arm
to suggest to us that all along
our form was only meat.

My flesh is an energy of figure,
    a tunnel of connected things
that begs to go on further.
Each of its pores may even be imagined
    a receptacle for nails,

its ears as sites for pins.
Here, now, the poem inspires
  no transformation
recall the arrow or song
to the trembling daylight
from which it sprang—
  but nothing springs,
the Egyptian sculptures, the Greek sculptures,
  the absent limbs of certain works,
unable to bring about even the slightest quiver
  in regions of feeling
that just before had trembled.

At the onset of new destructions
  unfathomable silence
this cannot be: it is.
A pit, and a painting of a pit.
And over there, the body.
Here the first world
  swallows up the second.

Knowledge of mortality
  yields up more
than fantasies of light.
Only by the violent X-ray of our satisfactions
  can excitation and dread
shatter the hand
that plagues us.

IV. Necessary Composition

My Dinner with Mingxia

In my backyard I have two trees.
One is an olive tree. The other
Is an olive tree too.

To please her boyfriend
A woman has the pattern of her lingerie
Tattooed in black ink onto her torso.

The cat is sitting on the tracks.
Her claws are in the window.

I speak in two languages.
You are hearing only the second one.

If it pleases my husband
I have two olive trees.
The other is also an olive tree.

I am of two tongues
like two otters slinking through the snow.

You should not smoke that cigar.
Its ash will melt the snow

I will have to worry about it later
when you are ill and lying in the snow.

Of we two, one is the more interested
in nudes. This lovely passage is an example.

Later, when your penis gets big
it will be tattooed on your skin in black ink.

Acrimony Garden, Garden Of Life

Garden plucked
   from the brow of the Creator.
Garden wrenched from the coils
   of rage.
Garden of raving,
    garden of chants.
Garden of tentacles
   of infinite reach.
Oleander garden in thickets of sun.
Acrimony garden, garden of life.
Garden of steeples,
    no sign of gods.
Garden of doubt
   in the snowdrifts.

Garden of soils. Garden of snakes.
Soul garden. Quince gardens.
Garden of flowers and purposeful thoughts,
garden of doorways, garden of stones,
manicured garden, minuscule garden,
miraculous garden of silence and stealth:
garden of boisterous blasphemous flesh.

Aromatic wheelchair garden.

Soapwort starling garden.

Ten thousand adjective garden.

Figurine garden, unicorn garden,
    pillared arcades enclosing a fragrance.
Spring, summer and fall flora

in simultaneous full flower and fruit.
Garden of rapids at the ridge
    of the falls.
Pomegranate garden, garden of lace.

Garden of afternoons
    before they are spoken.

Garden of mornings
    just as they're spent.

Dictating garden of lengthening dreams.

Belated garden of love and of taste.

Feature

This abundance, if it exists,
Is incompatible with constraint.

A culture unfurls from the perceptions
Avowed by this hypothetical, a primal history
Ties one to the elms of the most general of arguments
Unbound on all sides, overflowing with light
Like a river that threatens to inundate a fallow plain.

So these shores disperse their fictions, Indian arrow
And otherwise, angry variants of what remembered cliffs.

It bodes well for the present,
This acumen of the proximate soul,
Neither plastic calf nor generic recovery.

So here's upsurge
Vacillates on the horizon, mortar and brick
Migrating far off into the dreamscape
That a more difficult notation might stabilize
Here's foreground.

The earth is not a building but a body.

Difficult Passage

Though it corresponds with x, the portrait is already changing,
in a direction that was pointedly authorized well before,
when any of us were sovereign over what now is sublimated
        once; when thought was time.
And whenever this kind of undertow exacts itself,
there are many scenes played back for further clarification,
and the being of being-perceived is re-enacted,
this time from the inside of its rectangular shell.

Any point on such a time-line can be represented,
only this one point is not
neither x, nor not-x.
Yet detached from the official portrait
it can provide only a xerox of the past.
Like the dope wagon that was hooked onto the rest of the train,
fusing imperceptibly with all that was heading
                          in the one direction.
Or the Coke bottle, an emblem of the American way of life,
propagated in popular advertising all over the world,
filling with liquid from some other space.
This is the point at which a mattress rises from the surf,
        responsive to all signifiers.
It too is American.

Mostly, there are the minds that wake up in the morning
ready for action and untroubled by waves.
They say, no choice but the one that pretends there is choice —
a truth that does not hold for *Difficult Passage*.
In fact, nothing holds less at the margin of time.
Drop by drop it is the dismemberment of water
the lifting of foam
        section of the portrait. This is where we are,

this is it, now this. While we cannot summon
the coordinates of these our correspondences
the red dust on the floor boards shines more brightly
when the sun is finally centered.

Necessary Composition

for Michael Palmer

"To reverse a phrase of the anthropologist Fernandez, metaphor is not a plan for ritual but ritual may suggest a plan for metaphor and both ritual sacrifice and metaphor may be seen as integral to an economy of consumption." —David Pierce

"We shall begin with architecture: beginning with the beginning - *arche*." —Denis Hollier

The prison like a slowly filling notebook,
the bars almost imperceptible, and the inmates

so that each new sentence hardly seems to matter
and the daily entries, at first burning, restless,

become as chaos tamed by a house of chains, memory
bent double against the ivy,
     whispers in the house of bondage.

Or:

after architecture
     the screen was a temple
and each letter an offering.
     I have worshiped the towers
word by word so reconstructed.
     All that was seen
and all that was spoken
     opened creation to a new creation.

Other plans for metaphor:

Fire, the mistress
   to whom sacrifice
   is made, silver as change,
   unreadable as an electrified fence.

Howls of smoke.

Unrecognizable logs,
   men in uniforms standing guard.

Only the thinnest of representations
   allows for the experience.

❧❧❧❧❧❧❧❧❧❧

Surely the body stands in need
of its expression in architecture?
Bed is not architecture
but the edifice is born

The demiurge of co-production
left in control
of its towers and walls.

The snow is swept from the stoop
and the door man dreams:
A Bastille in no way different
from its own storming.

Come then the real pleasures of this prison —

Consumption and void.

But if all architecture is also assembly
in overflow of determinate function,

poem without purpose,

the slabs between pronouns
and the wreckage on the platform

must then be performing
indeterminate functions

the revelation of which only takes place
once history has ended.

Contrary to popular belief
this has yet to be achieved.

Confusion and Ecstasy, then, as cultural moments.

Ecstasy?
To die without dying?
When even the snow
is tired of snowing ?

Snow-mounds.

A furnace, a house of fire.

A Venusberg in Furs.

You are growing
fatigued with this.

For many moments —
for long stretches —
I no longer have the slightest idea.

꒔

The moment after she removed her clothes:

Chain-link fence encircling a slaughterhouse,
    fish net stockings slipped over some meat.

Ceaseless vibration of stain glass
eyes, lidded, moored below the forehead.

The eye dwells among the manufactured things
and the voice manufactures the vision.

They emigrated further and further into the snow,
    until they stumbled upon a museum
filled with Francis Bacons'.

Yes, *architecture is frozen music*
as he raises his voice to the rafters

The work of spirit passing from mineral to phrase
through the mediation of song, however mutilated
    singer and mouth.

As for the would be builders of ancient Babel,
    I ask you — masters or slaves?

(Only the slave could write
        the history of confinement.
    But only the master would have
        the time to read it.)

Mnemosyne, the lyric mode of production —
        how the slave revamps her body.
Cemeteries unearthed. Pyramid and Sphinx.

It that gives the words
        commands the labor —
to have chosen a devotion
        to Echo,
    the promise
        that each phrase is a palimpsest,
a little opening to a greater clamor,
        the actual objects of thought.

                    🦅

1) *It felt like sitting on a burning cigarette*
        but something good came of it:
        a screaming child.

2) We'd built an igloo of flesh
        and still, the sun melted it.

3) Poetry as the failure of architecture.
    Bricks that died to make heaven
            shrink to earth.
    Horizontally, the thread that leads into the labyrinth
            of the intestine, as at a butcher's shop
            or the intimate church.

Its methods as original as ground

The "unconscious" and the "conscious" is a vertical construction

Horizontally

It was as if the stripper had remained dressed
    after removing her clothes -
    her flesh glowed hard and soft at once

    You could and you could not see

    The stretched center of the room

    The cage and the structure
    that gives birth to the cages

    Eye that allows you

    Inside
    and outside
    at once

    A deep plush violent pink

    Object of desire
    in dissolve after dissolve

At *Wall to Wall Sex,*
production-house of want

    Could and could not speak

Necessary Composition   59

The writhing request
of the writing not to be left

Pushed it open with my fingers
: a moisture on the text.

Warm blood drawn
from the neck of the beast.

Everything that is solid
melts into
Metaphor.

For example, the signpost over the ruined store front
on Water Street that reads:
The Endless Construction Company.

Not new life but
sacrifice, consumption.

After creation,
and before the mind

the red-light district and
the industrial district are one

that Desire and Imagination need overcome

not by immolation but by writing

— rewriting —
a thing without walls

invisible columns upholding the vertical.

Fake Abdication

So much worth destroying
to begin destroying makes no sense.
So I just go forward with my everyday affairs,
without evident irony or active anger
towards the objects of my rage,
hoping that the edifice I pile up above me
allows my better self to mount.
I repeat, there is no hope of winning.
The largesse of this vale
defies any set of measurements
the head can ever hope to stage.
I take it the words have acted
upon the dried out landscape until it is inhabitable,
but next day the land is just as foreign
and there are fewer words with which to try.
People gradually lose the capacity to curse, subside back
to the animal state that can't, or else curse
so gratuitously that it too seems animal.
Here come some of my loud friends now,
speaking without thinking,
crying out in joyous freedom from their brains,
choking on food as their nervous systems unfurl -
unwinding after a long day.
What is this burly thing pressing in all around us
but the proof of our own passing away?
My mind is made up, I will not roar back.
There is no drowning out what one is drowning in.
Count out my share of the draught if it must be
something contested, though I will drink what is given.
To be blockaded by the most trivial of things
grown into a monster. What was it Artaud once said?
Here I must ask you to scream.

Slumber, Party, and *Frisson*

"A booth of cement" it might be called, or "an abyss separating the past from the future", or perhaps "a terrible rip in the word-play": these, the rhythms of my rhetoric, defy even my own capacity for self-reflection. The abstract thicket grows. Once again to return to a void neither absence nor appearance, neither perception nor speech, a blanket statement treadmilled to infinity. The mind conscious of its deadly repetitions, all the same trapped by these self-same repetitions, taking on bilge, allowing itself to sink, retracing the same proffered commands, gravelly comments and stammers. Pools of percussion do sometimes break in to provide mildly interruptive interludes, lifting up my leaden face by beating down on tautened textiles and skins, muffled pulsations and echoes insisting my metabolism alter its habitual rhythms, move out of itself. Taken to its logical extreme such soundings would mean that the body is the pathway to God. Yet cries at the window are also influential, tires spinning on the sheeted streets also fashion consuming tales. From the other room a voice chips in: "turn off the track-lights, the radiance streaming through the windows will now be sufficient". And all the dust flying in that one shaft of sunlight? "Bundle it onto the outback". That is dust's purpose: to be evenly distributed across a vast plain until the whole of the expanse is finally coated by that which light first revealed as ancillary to itself, as an afterthought, as utterly unnameable. So the tiniest detail of Being, grandly proclaiming its ascendancy, gums up the works; from the dust we emerge, to the dust we return. Pit of torpor, fill instead with assertions of being? Fumbled hours, stand up like a trumpet blowing notes? How? To what end? I am something vaster than myself. Meaning: I cannot remember all that I am. This is only one example.

༺

The recreational blizzard of the emotions,
run-off passions of a blind day —

The capacity to remember other ways of seeing it, a thought fanning outwards in concentric circles, line miraculously transmitted across bristling rivers of space. Depending on the tide, the flow of the river alters directions, transporting the herds of floating ice to one of two imaginary points. This is not an analogue for memory, exactly, but rather an exhortatory tale, something to shoot for. For cast into a world alien from its conception, the aspiring self can only hope to reimagine every aspect of its home, or else abort its mission with one primeval act. Sacrosanct, this final alternative, and guaranteed of success, however disappointing to others. While along the first route, one runs the risk of a mere puttering around, a strictly delimited mental landscape abounding with signaled boundaries and clumsy cues warning you when to pull back, when to retreat inside your shell of imagined reality — if such a retreat is not inevitable, it is at least the prevalent mode of existence among most of us today. The capacity to remember other ways of doing it, fanning outwards in concentric circles, occupying the miraculous landscape, making of the intersected world a muscle responsive to triple massage - not only the beating wings of birds, not only the productive furnaces and chips, but my own sense of being as it swells and eddies as well. To take the object back, to make it human — a failed project whose conclusion is endlessly repeated, one which all the same warms the heart beating inside the protective conch of morning, far from the forces that shape and design the contours of each waking, wondering how to leave the early hours for the late, how to walk out the door into the dark of the century. If Non- Being is the more perfect solution, a life devoted to perplexity remains the more daring.

If the years are seen as passing in unremitting and outrageous single file, leaving one to wonder how it came to be that one hadn't grasped their meaning even as they trooped so visibly by, then the time has come to clear your desk of everything, take a deep breath, and write your local Commissar a letter. "Dear Sir", the letter should begin, "I am dying." This simple declarative sentence is all that will be neces-

---

sary to draw his attention. After that the writing can grow densely packed, rich with textures and plateaus, as elegant a form of address as the reader for whom it is intended. Yet "the Commissar" makes this reader sound so official, no doubt officiousness was the point behind that particular word choice, enough to say you entrust yourself to him, you grant the reader a say in your own survival. As the letter deepens it will become possible to forget this dependency, to embellish upon new and greater agencies of formal rapture, converting everything into literary structures, phantasms braced for the coming of a cold blast of remorse. Come inside now, it is already too chilly to remain outside without a shirt and long pants. Come to your desk, to your unfinished letter, the one I have demanded you write for me. Make your bed if you think that will help, only impose some kind of order on the *vagabondage* of your anger, arrive at a more law-like but less predictable happenstance of thought. And while it remains infuriating to each of us to posit a reader, then feel the syllables pouring out onto the writing table totally unobserved, one can still be thankful that these words are not consumed, made into a part of the reader as would be brussels sprouts, since just such disappearances were the threat which brought you to go out into the desert with your clothing all askew to speak with strangers in the first place. Like the momentary freezing of the eyes when someone has suddenly grasped that all is not quite right with you, a look that just as quickly your interlocutor will attempt to hide. Too late. You have seen his terror surface and then go under — just so, one's appearance cannot be digested — and this was precisely the catch you had in mind, the silver flash of shock and recognition, the ordinary becoming the strange. What is the mechanism of alarm, and when it is sounded, how does it play amongst us, refining into something more profound? "If you're not scared 60% of the time, you're not alive", the poet once said. And as the crowd files out of the amphitheater and the aisles jam in orderly silence, the ability to live with fear — but also to draw sustenance from it — gradually increases.

All forms are fragile
when countered by force

none there are that can withstand
the pressure of time

in the shape they were before
in the shape they meant to stay

And so memory is scattered to multiform
stamps and their entertaining faces

Stripped from the envelope
dried of their mucilage

a family of nations
passing over your fingertips

one's share of reality hinged to the pages
gathered in one book

the traces of messengers
crushed to the same canvas.

The Clearing

Space and sleep   each branch off
into alternate solitudes   as terminal as bone.
But it is there all along, the greater space,
to leap to, to look up and along at

breaking off from objects into light.

The cloud disperses. There, that's so much better. But how might one keep off opacity in a more controlled and permanent way, that Being might more frequently brush against itself? And what is left after the heaviness has passed? It is more the shape of a cat curled in sleep on a chair than the shape of a snake eating its own tail, more the urge towards silence of a winter night than the clarion call of a decision. "You have lived in the expectation of some startling recompense", the poet continues, and now one wonders: is this that day? Will all be revealed? Is the curse going to be lifted, and as the fruit of metaphorical actions I have taken along the way? One will never be able to say. There was no appropriation in the budget with which to ground an inquiry, no slacking off in the mystery of sensation. So an undifferentiated rant in the heart of desire gives way to a purposeful singling out of particular infinites, an endless regression is converted into a pulsating star. And even if the tiny anxieties in the petri dish of the present can never be induced to let up or go away, even if the rumor of my future disintegration is already beginning to disseminate among the toll-takers and ne'er do wells of the years to come, this, my waking life, remains alluring. The compensation is in the wondering, in the making it up and seeing it happen, in the dark opacity of a bar of chocolate placed before me on the table. Although all the significant inscriptions remain outside the power of understanding and memory, although there can never be any authentic accommodation to an alien slope of manufacture and consumption, I am here as much as a man on a chair-lift is ever the cable.

⤺

To shift from one perspective to the next loosens up the musculature of being. This loosening is sometimes called "breathing", other times, "listening", other times "the one who lies beside you". A cycle of intimacies leads one forward through hostile rings, those mutinous archons that separate oneself from the possible. Things flutter, the plates that underpin the objects of one's affection are abruptly felt to slide. Each phrase added to the humus. Each sentence an abstraction except if taken with the whole. If the embouchure of poetry is a positioning of the total organism in which this self-same figure is also the instrument to be blown through and eventually played, then another day has been entirely wasted. Despair is sacred, but the moment this is realized, we cease to despair.

V. New Poems

High Tide

Islets of a quandary only solved by plunging into the sea.

To fathom this geography periscopes must supersede
The dry eye's intuitions.

But it is these very specks of ground we choose to cling to.
The barren rocks are licked by waves and seem
Less barren if we see those waves as passion.

Such mystery is greater than anything we can hope
To locate in the minutia of our circumstance:
Shore gives way to plain gives way
To mountain gives way to plain and timid shore.

So passion holds us in our places even as it
Intimates its source is a place so liquid as to stand
Outside place, where nothing stands, where
Everything rolls, a ritual cognition towards which
We work, roiling in the beds of given language.

I want to see where I came from but to be where I stand.

In the next round of coming-to-awareness
We can assure ourselves that such balance will be possible.

Rolling on the bed sheets of anticipation
Each breath is listened for as it gives away
A passage of air, a mimetic of persistence.

The wind-swept, wave-swept rocks,
A coast line pelted by the daemonic force
Of the ocean that surrounds it, mystery
That drips of salt . . . an old man in a yellow rain slicker.

This ritual of cognition fixes us to a certain knowledge.
From inside the blood stream periscopes supersede
The irises intuitions, but these are not cognitions,
They are cold sweats, eruptions in identity
Deemed impossible but inhabited by sickly clouds.

An old man in a yellow rain slicker, at home looking out

But then he turns towards us and yells up for directions.
His next utterance is drowned out by a thunderclap.

The longer you wait to respond to these signs
The harder it will be to hold back the unnameable gush
Of emotion when the ocean can no longer be withstood.

These islets are so little you can literally hop
From one to the next and only if you slip
Will your pants get brined and your sneakers
Licked by the minnows and weeds off the coast.

The next perception is blinded in a flash of lightening
And the line after that is drowned out in a thunder clap
And after that comes the wind, always the wind
Walloping the windows with the collective force
Of a nature you have never yet allowed your being to confess.

Your body is subject to it all the same.

The storm is an extension of the sea.
The sea is an extension of the maternal.

It is building in intensity, but not
Towards a climax: it is the awareness
Of an intensity that precedes climax.

The rage of the storm is a blank check
On which we inscribe the figure we think
Will underwrite the most damage the crashing waves
Are likely to create along the fragile beach head.

The sea is a quandary of words and figures
That encroaches on our most complete moments
Of emptiness and insists we fill that emptiness
And be filled and build and be built
Until the islet seems a populous hub.

The only balance in the offing is propagation.

Paolo and Francesca

Flexible waves, sprays flung when we are
Wholly sex, open wounds of love
To pleasure without remorse for wounds.

This is the chemical exchange of the self
For more powerful patterns of contact in the blood:
The body releases its drug as the hurt eases.

Takes flesh to know flesh but god and goddess to spasm:
Time lapse photography reveals no change in form
Since this body remains unphotographable, as we know.

We broke off from our reading of the book.
We put down what never could be put down.
We turned to each other, blinded by what we'd read.

Adorned by nothing but our breasts
The fluidity of weight brandished as a weapon
Against a culture of signs.

Out of the hell of the libidinal head
Dead rise of doves that are forever
Blood oranges in a basket. In the sun.
                    The fibers glistening.

So moved by our lives
We could not any longer utter the design-to-excite
So lightly carried by the wind.

Mundus Nominalis

In our cell drawn by the perimeter of darkness
We have observed namelessness to assume a certain form.

Though the favored elixir, the one that fuels a euphoric
Rush of sensation, does not waterfall into a diction

Equal to the external circumstances -
Circumstances here are simply too external -

The outline of a shape that might be a phrase,
Its movement as stealthy as that of a coyote,

As a quartet of coyotes silently communicating,
Radiates from a distance a thin vibration of intelligence.

By the very act of asking the alien to name itself
We are inscribing an intricacy we can never duplicate

In a zone beyond our linguistic ardors
In which vaporous seeds plant the fruit of contradiction

These perceptions of curtain and field,
Of the things themselves in passing.

A sharper cross-roads claims us for its own.
Precision, like a loud bang, shuts off the lights.

Map

for Mary Margaret Sloan and Joseph Donahue

The old world's roadwork
wrapped in the wax paper of mouldering seas:
the soaked and blossoming trees of an island.

Festival flickers, ecstatic footage islanders suggest
To an intruding film maker, until the intruder is
Touched by the festival . . . a dance about three volcanoes.

And the soaking trees have a daughter
Afoot before me, a woman of weighted motion,
    joyful in the silence of things.

Her world without wound is the carnivore withheld.
In the forest of euphoria I met my tropical twin.
A book bound at the volcano's edge flows away with the lava.

The sun's stone lifts itself to enroll a mortuary blaze
and then the stone - our earth -
    turns away from its own vision.

彡

Primordial finger tips
lift no cloud of enfolded dawn:
a city morgue chills in the lunar jag.

A strange actor, all ribs, knowing only one cadence,
seeks the sun-god,
streaks of filth lining his glasses.

It is too early.

Creation waved on
passed my outpost like a funereal limo.
Exile itself blackened out by millennial words.

It is too early.

Manhattan carries Eros in by her hair
and the carnage around me
is given a spire to peg it:

"Shore leave", "the sailor
and his silver", "sperm puddles",
the material gist of material tides

Love's pull unglossed by any map.
This city's predatory gaze.
A green beer bottle on the counter's formica edge.

(Speechifying in sun-lit squares
the stranger seeks out moon-lit gullies.
He sleeps in moon-lit gullies.)

Adam exists only in that bone
spliced from out of the past,
now fluorescent.

Propped between brightness and grime
in a barrel bobbing towards hell,
the earth twists, the light still blockaded behind it.

The sun hovers over the battlefield,
    shaking its burning spells,
And the warriors, sweating, are part of that spell.

Or the sky transports a light never seen before,
gold cheeks of the dancing star.
The fighters, the fishermen, all will look up.

A woman of weighted motion,
joyful in the silence of things,
spreads out a magnificent atlas.

If only ecstasies could be exhumed
from their bodies graves,
the syllables of distinct strata of experience

Might conjoin over daybreak.
If only wrinkles on the map gave birth to islets
Dots of magma might be formed from these engravings.

Map

75

Poem

for David Shapiro

The light hangs me in the light
but that is not
what I came for.
I'd wanted something lighter.

Light suffuses the patios of the poor
from the train to Pisa light bathed
the flowers in the window boxes of the poor
and that comes closer but not quite.

The thought of delivering light to the very cells,
of shining a light into matter
and saying yes, yes this is it,
I see it now, the light

Sensible at its very source,
there it is at work.
Even lighter than that.
Getting the hang of life.

Year One

"The isolate satyr each man is"
—Robert Duncan

It strikes me that this is a dimension of stillness
I have not visited before —

Those lulls that take hold between giddy exhortations to life,
The ones that hold you briefly in their fledgling embrace —

Only this stillness is as wide as a church organ
And as big as the heart of the grape.

To finally be open to the fullness of being
Without any duplication of the fullness before

In a new intoxication anticipated by all the others
But not sounded until now,

A music imprinted on the air around you
With an intensity that makes the air vibrate

Beyond its point of origin
To a place in the universe origin could never contain

Actualized as a chord by an organ
That energizes the points in the ear

Until creation breaks from its chains into a grin
It too drunk on the best of Bacchus.

꙾

You hear each note as if for the first time.
You look around the room as if at living coral.

And what you see makes you never want to leave
Never want to return to the choppy surface you left behind

Since the fish and the spines are here so colorful
So perfectly integrated with the sea

You cannot tell the difference between where
Their lives and their art leave off —

Less a painting than a kind of music,
Rhythmic, endless, oceanic feeling

As near as you can tell undisturbed
By a life of habitual aggression

The killer forgetting that he's killed,
Agave unaware of her son's head on the spear

And so what if my view is filtered by such dislocation,
It is still a view, it is a paradise I have seen

I have heard and continue to hear amply even now,
The precise marble pyramid which catches my eye

Marble of which vicious Rome was built,
Carrara on the piano colored coffee table

The legs of which mimic a panther's paws
And some unrecorded temple of the god

It is extraordinary that all this began in a stillness
That was no doubt available to me all along

That I want you to know I still hear
Even if words must always belie it

Even if I can't get these words to float on it,
To rest on cushions before the glory of.

That is the skill reserved for the great ones
For whom "impassioned" and "still" are not contradictions

That is the skill reserved for the immortals
Who sing of a union between logos and song

Well beyond our broken abilities to build
Union into our acts of art and love

So much to the margin of the central contradictions
That mark our lives as our's.

And yet
the stillness demands we offer ourselves to it

Risk the folly of moving to the music,
Of forwarding words before the articulate

Into the contaminated air that beats them
Until something awful to comprehend

Only this lull in the drinking is as wide as a church organ
And as big as the heart of the grape

Words Before the Articulate

It is a cyclops we wish to build
And if a cyclops has only one eye

The monocular vision is the more unitary sign
It is the cyclops of a flower

Simply simply don't let this watering ever cease

Book of J
for David Rosenberg

Installed
at the crossroads of coincidence

A declaration
which imprints
on the pell-mell

The voice of J, J's insinuation
in nebulous languages, shapes.

"*Eion,* dissembler,

but also the finite

faced by the infinite,

an infinite, as it turns out, that is impish."

(If texts are false origins
sliced out of chance
still, they are starting points.)

"Breath" spat into "clay"

These words are ironic

With irony no creator,
no reader, ever is self-identical.

The gardens are sweetly fornicated one after another —

Irony of the circling zoos, irony of
the stable, then scattered, foundations

Incommensurate after incommensurate handshake.

Irony lends dignity to unleavened bread —

Irony narrows the eye in its crag
And fills the "I think" with "I think" —

Irony *is against Nature's increase*
Under irony no idea is allowed to spread
    No ideas but in irony
Listen, Pound
Power here garners no gain from its pressure

Irony has the atom cutter contaminated
    by the product of his labor

Adam's red clay, that first solitary spring.

Their misreading of "tree"
demonstrated that "tree" had faded as a source

After which their mortal form became instantly visible;
    each carved
his or her heavy name back into the trunk.

Here is the scroll of uncertainty,
        Yahweh
the speaker whose context is redacted

"a few buckets of water,
        tied up in a complicated sort of fig leaf."

So consciousness keeps singing its mimetic pun
   in case books belie it

The articulate leaps of a startled angel anywhere present

Lets me drink the beads dripping down the stalk.

Episodes from a Possible *Nekyia*

Keep in mind
each noun,
   as it is found lacking,
reverts to its precursor state,
   said the ferryman
but nothing further

Fluid foundation of the river
he was averred to have ridden,
as if rafting were precursor
   to writing,
certainly the raft of image
tied together by these tilled
   tendrils and cords:

As if composition
were going to take me
   out beside Charon's fiction,
blue sky's flash into undifferentiated
   foundations of place,
I ask so much of Nothingness
nothingness is inured to my asking
(it is posed all the same) :

That I be blended into the boundary of my pursuit

Outside my own usage
  undigestible data   along Awe's direct route

A divine dolphin circling the firmament.

"A WRIT is a route" —Gerrit Lansing

Possible experience,
its rim so gradually circled
the circular motion is not even sensed.

Rim from which
  one gazes over a precipice
of sheer imagination,
  of scandalous end -

Rim from which
  the ground may vanish,
the petrified path give way,
and then one is hiking in the song,
  hiking on hiking,
air saturated with ichor's fiction.

A thorn to remind me of what I am,
the particular stuff to which I cling.
Trekking since sunrise
where a straight road has never been -
  fiery red stain splashed over the rim -
and dark was falling now
  and all I'd seen was rocks.

Yet anything could happen
  out there,
that "anything" the product
  of a unique human formation -
That is, not quite
  free,
not quite dependent
but a constant exposure
of matter at the thought-tip —

Episodes from a Possible *Nekyia*   85

Dusty trails
    swarming with ghosts,
gate-keepers in the splintered cliffs,
a population of partial steps
    shivered into half-achieved
riffs in the landscape,
    would-be, could-be, might-have-been
quiver of phantasms slung on one's back,
the path littered with shattered sticks
    that once might have been pointed
and now they were not.

This rim is
    available experience,
unpossessed if not carefully composed,
    circled slowly,
tending towards union
    because tended towards union,
even if the unyielding landscape
    says it is otherwise.

Asking the "tavern keeper"
    to say otherwise,
brandy washing over
    my broken cleft.
Waiting for
    the next morning's wanderings.
Outside is rock, looking at rock,
    watching some rocks,
listening for water.

The dead in the song
Whose sticks of names
Rise in the charred smoke
What seeds in whose remains
Brewing themselves in continual thirst

It is the song that remembers
He constructs as he is burned
(An angel begs to be whipped
Wishing to distract us with his antics
Because run out of words)

So X rings out to be renamed
That under her lobe she wore
A pearl kindled as we watched
She was lust like of sun
We were viable clay
Yielding anthropos by the ray

Something more than the wailing angel
Alive in the sticks
Syllables these are
Looped into a bezelled instrument
Like flame

Singed reeds to conjugate the lungs
Breath that is vocable shoots unbound
In so many diaphragms the voices sprout

Dew flicked from the blossom.

Or:
The blossom,
An organic body, continually burns

And fire sermons
    become tradition.

So that the grind of avenues chews up my matter:

The song knows of what it speaks
As soot creeps through the loose folds of the coats
Charred smoke seeks charmed smoke
Seeks charmed snake in the garden
Smoke of the smoke black as the burnt
Finds nothing where nothingness
    might have been charmed
Only was charnel.

Everything here desirable will yet be consumed.

The demiurge
Directs our attention down avenues of delay.
I enter Loiterers Cafe
    and I order.

ٮ

Something torn apart,
      no doubt by the war,
allows the forms to rip
Aflutter on the air —
   feasting on the golden wounds
   his bruised body offers,
the molten metal of Hephestes flows
down the painter's throat, killing him
   with its weight,
if not with its weight,
   then its heat,
And he didn't die, he was opened.

What he didn't die of
      was monument
to what he was,
      was rock, was quarry,
a vein of divinity
      opened to itself
definitively by Mars, the painter dying
in a field, a suffering mine
      to be mined for suffering,
his chest blown apart
the world enters to rush away
and he didn't die, he was opened.

The true colors of Europe's woods,
      the buildings of the old world
made rubble by the bombs,
And a new god entering
      the painter's chest
asking him to stay alive,
      showing him how
to make breath out of gold

Episodes from a Possible *Nekyia*   89

and blood out of shrapnel
as in the old days
before they'd killed or driven underground
    the alchemists
and held our noses to the grindstone.

He saw all the deep colors
floating above like newborn stars,
    furtive planets
sprinkled across the viscous heaven
    of his chest in ribbons,
his stomach oozing out
over the inky blue night
identical with naked soil.
    Lying among the dead
He was open to the inchoate form
of his own organs without form,
the chaos of a head
unheralded by any mental order
because there was none:
    no head, no order, no herald
he was dying,
Andre Masson would always be ecstatically dying
    from that night forward . . .

for Simon Carr

꙳

Words Before the Articulate

Patterns of sun and mist
    over the palisades,
Mist moving to seaward
And the sun — the sun
Hidden now in tissues of cloud.
The goddess dances on the cliff,
    long limbed, barely clad,
Her skin *cafe au lait* colored, alluring.
Such I am allowed to see
And I ask no more than the sight,
The mist like a serpent
    writhing down the cleft of the river,
The sky a concealed friction.
Man is passive when he gazes
    but active when he gazes
At the goddess by her command,
The attributed landscape as lithe
    as the spell of her movements,
As sinewy as earliest spring:
"Active" as in "votive", "votive" as in "pit",
    "pit" as in "attunement
To the fictive."

The transformations the sun accomplishes
    disappear an instant later.
A hump in the mist
    rises to a peak
And then rejoins the lower rush.
Temporally, spatially, the mind is a flux
Verging on the invisible, yet polychromatic.
Temporally, spatially, my body rises on the bank
To observe the elements, however my own distillation
From elemental muck confuses that regard.
So the dark goddess shapes her dance

On the banks behind the consumer city,
Bares herself to the collective eye of the laborers
Whose offerings she depends on,
To whom she offers relief from the labor.
She asks her devotees to find new ways
     to speak of her, to her,
To sensitize their tongues,
To learn a cursive script
With which to address the naked.

Showers broke over my speech,
      refreshed the lagoons
as speech played the flute in the ruins
I hadn't before noticed I stood in.

So that I didn't get out,
 couldn't go under, wouldn't run away,
let the rain make its haven
over the motionless heron in my heart —

This fluid foundation of marsh
      oozing with matter   thunder drops
blind burst by blind burst penetrating thick soup
while the flute like a throat
bespoke the ruins of glades had been endless
      and now they were not.

Something the shower was sending,
something more than a wailing angel
      alive in the sticks,
speech not as shelter but species being:
      and I wept in the slough
for the very source of diversity,
the magic of language in its differential spell,
this bird-filled lagoon in which
      words would be brewing new tropes
if only we were receptive.

The mind: a calling
on the threshold of the inaudible,
polyvocal in its desire
to speak with itself.

"The opening of the organism to take in
        the world around it,"
Duncan writes —

". . . recapitulating the experience of those first cells of life in the
primal waters."

Up to my waist in that Florida catch basin,
the mangroves twined around an invisible beam,
when the flute trilled again from the dark:

This water must be waded,
these cells cannot wait.
Gnosis begins in primary trouble.

꒰꒱

Flammable float
burns up in the current
until a lash of smoke
twisted over Styx
is all that can be seen
by the immigrant hawk
a mile overhead.

From my own perch
I saw a ball of silver cloud
continue to roll
oceanward,
conceived the dead to depart
with no other form
than this orb
the hawk
— alien to all smoke —
could not talon seize.

A certain intellectual freedom—

Funny how we strain
    to grasp reality
and then find it
    in such suspect reveries.

For those in the trailing wisps,
    it was too late.
They were signaling to us the lateness
    as they left.

A certain intellectual freedom —

Everything is from elsewhere,
    goes elsewhere,

and can only be located
    by getting elsewhere
in the mind.
Hawk transported
    from some distant region.
Columns of the Fort Tryon cloister,
        the cloister itself,
transplanted
    stone by stone
to the bank
    to which I've wandered,
a building that bears witness
        to an opposite time,
an "I" displaced in its very surroundings.

Transported too
the scriptorium:
I distinctly recall myself
as having there written
    "ferry mam" for "ferry man"
in an earlier version
— each noun reverts
        to its precursor —

And then I'd aborted it

Insisting that the flaw in creation
    was the creation
superimposed back upon
    the creative ecstasy
from which it was spawned.

"Pity me
whatever you are,
shade or living man",

pleads what you are
to what
you might yet have
the power to make.

Breath and pulse shudder
   at light's implication.

ᵏ˕

Are you getting what you need?
   asked the parrot
and she would not land.
Are you getting what you need?
   asked the parrot,
green wings spread wide,
   her eye a provocation.
Are you getting what you need?
   and her plumes
grew moist with honey.
Are you getting what you need
Are you getting what you need?

The warmth
   the lady creates
precedes the first man
   to feel that warmth
the central fact
   of his inner life.

Or a snake resting on a blanket
   completely at ease
but no, his coils are tensed:
tensed but at ease
only the first of his contradictions.

At the command
   of the coffee colored goddess
this serpent writhes along the river's cleft
for as far as the eye can see.

It hunts smoke and cloud
   and when it finds them
it constricts them in its flesh,
   beads of dew condensing on its coils.

When sun warms the scriptorium
   in which it lives
the mind stirs, the throat grows active
   as the mist clears.

A certain
freedom of the moment —

To sit in the sun
neither the sun
nor the sitter
but an amalgam
of perceptions at work
between beings
the sun and the sitter
are grounds of.

Evolution of forms:
The solar perplexed.

The prospect of a future sighting
   from this foothold
in the present.

Hawk, serpent, and mimetic bird —
pneumatics in defiance of undefiable Styx.

O you in that little bark
What is the relation of the painting to its title

The painting bears no relation to its title
The tiny boat bears

nameless people across
water that is infinitely dark

—Michael Palmer

A pale boat,
a pale man paddling it,
advancing steadily from the other shore.
 I saw the white boat,
     I saw it
skimming towards Donahue's mother,
the boat man himself,
earnest, grim, intrepid.

He did not lift the boat
    out of the water.
He did not put the boat
    onto his back and walk past her
into the field.
He beckoned to her,
    and she came.
When he gestured like that
    she had to go.
They went.

The painting bears no relation to its title

Name infused by flesh

The painting bears no relation to its title

But I'd learned her name
    before she left:

O you in that little bark

Portent between sunlight and mist
Grows lustrous in the union

Not as in discontinuous, dissonant loss
But as in the unwinding clarification of the river.

↜

Cut in the unspoken
    cliff —

Lyric undergrowth
   encircles the entrance
to this break in the limestone.

Freshly discovered
not by search but by
     patience,
a mind unfazed by its fictions,
    a moan
unconnected to anything mirrored,

Open only to those
    alert, this desire
to enter the interstices,
to feel one's way
    forward through "perhaps".

Rustling of bats
    like angels at the entrance.
Entanglements of shrub
    that somehow survive
with little available sun.
Cramped corridor leads
    to a chamber,
its cavernous expanse,
while a horn sounds
   from a further hall,
asking me to stray further,
to seek solace in this surge,
   to consider staying,
rocks locked around one another

as if in embrace,
invisible waters trickling down
    ice-smooth warm walls.

Half expecting the Sibyl
    in folds of impassioned flesh
to ask me to shout, to refract her voice
       or mine
down the multiple perforations,
    honeycomb of caverns
further and further subdividing
    our cries into echo.
Nobody here to greet me?
Anticipating their faces
    on the verge of thronging forth.
But there is just the one instrument,
its soft wail
    from some further reach,
requesting a call in return
    in a medium so fluid
I haven't yet learned
    to there stay afloat.

Cut in the unspoken cliff —

A path inside the mountain face
that leads to a carpet of sand.
Edge of an underground pool
    in which nothing lives,
or in which there is nothing alive
    that yet wants to be seen.
Bare cracks of light,
elegant shafts
    touching the water.

Ceiling too just barely in view,
a relief from the narrow passage
    I remember just forging.
Funny how memory suddenly fails us.
Passages I could never retrace.
The cry of the horn —
    or is it a flute? —
haunting my movements,
    unmapping each space.

No idea
how to cross this catch basin/well.
Picked up a rock,
  pocketed it for later.
Waited for a bat,
  waited for a snake,
waited for an eagle.
Listened to the water
  trickle through the limestone.
The flute —
  or was it a chorus of flutes —
grew more insistent
  until the chamber walls
seemed to pick up the note,
undulated subtly to all sides
of the impermissible "I"
  lodged in its midst.

Or else that chord was a tremor
  in the earth's roots,
the unspoken core moaning from its remove
as my hand ran along
the smooth gushing sides
  of her cavern.

Vein of divinity
   opened to itself?
Quaking stone
   responsive to the touch.
Wet rock
   awaiting the next stroke.
A whole being enveloped
   by a thunderclap
come from underneath,
interior, vocable
   as clean as a wave.

"Or maybe this
is the sacred"

"To dream true, to figure true, to come true"

"And they will find me there
   and they will live,
and they will not die again"

"And the earth will again
   become part
of the primeval ocean"

These are the phrases attuned to
   entering the fluid,
sensing the salt,
   decentered by hunger
and the tide-flow of stars.

꜀

Since the noun seeks
   to be a verb.

Since the river
   is higher than the sky
and brackish as its color may be,
   it is still coursing,
still insistent on a direction,
   a progress towards no point
but the next revolution of its waters.

An epic of dissolving genres
   this dream we prefigure
of reality, this passion we prefigure
   of full passion,
reading as a manner of entering
   an underground pool
somehow linked to the sea.

An Emperor preparing his own tomb while still in good health.

All the paper that piles up in that archive in the tower.

Vast wealth of Kings, jade and alabaster accoutrements to life.

Vast wealth of phrases, marks on the paper.

Tomb amongst the parking lots.

Alive, the writer arranges for his own embalming.

His words are marched directly to the archive.

Alive, the writer sacrifices large pieces of his life in order to write.

His dream is to live on in his words.

The rest is death.

The archive beckons.

The archive is an abstraction.

The writer tells the embalmer to prepare his solutions.

One might say: "memory is all, poetry a single epic that preserves its own path."

One might say: "these people are delusional."

One might say: "lyric contagion figures an absolute delirium, an alternative means".

One might say: "that delirium is the only means".

One might say: "create yourself a soul, or else face oblivion."

One might smile at the old writer and the care with which he pre-
pares his own wrappings. But the emperors are remembered.

One might smile at the poverty of the writer's spoils, the paltriness of
his papers. But his work required no slaves.

By force of authority he hopes to pass himself on but not by force of
absolute authority.

No one was killed; some few were aided.

One might say: "he lives on as commodity, an object of knowledge."

One might say: "this commodity is a reification of his body".

One might say: " only ecstasy reveals the skein of the actual".

One might say: "fever of first expectation, disintegration of last
mind".

The archive keeps it all dry.

Far more interesting than the archive is the voyage to Lethe.

Yet it is the archive preserves the voyages to Lethe.

Far more interesting to travel to Styx, to return to the living elated.

But Styx runs through the archive.

Memory is all.

Point on the mortal planet
    into which
the rest of the planet
coils, tenses: from which
the planet prepares its strike
    at heaven

And the reader has just flicked off his light
and the book is still firm between his hands

As the train

pulls into the station.

Three dancers on the darkened train platform,
a muscular male
holding an unfamiliar instrument
    pressed to his lips:

On the other side of my sleeper's window
the dead in the song
whose sticks of names
rise in the charred smoke

They're gone by the time I exit.

Faces chipped from marble
    as one walks down the platform,
stone owls standing watch from the facade
    as one enters the deserted hall.

Gold-plated funereal bracelet encased to one side
    of a poorly lit space.

Udjat eye glaring from a pendant, measuring me.

Cobra known as Netjer-ankh
　　I'd read about once in a book
allows for the next apparition.

And a recumbent wooden jackal
　　up on a shrine —
I pass this imposing Anubis
and find, disturbingly,
I'm back at the Udjat eye.

Jade chimera,
　　its mouth gaping.
Jade dragon,
　　its coils dragging.
Jade disk,
　　they call it a "bi",
perforation at its center
　　posing a question
I wasn't even
　　conscious of thinking,
phantasms demanding
　　greater and greater
mandate,
　　a fluid foundation
lucid/opaque
　　in which to evolve.

Appears again the figure of Anubis.

Like a passage one reads again and again
without ever grasping:

Chained to my phantom,
    locked in my skin,
the book a dark tunnel
    protecting the book

Holding pattern
    of beauty without power
by which my feet are prevented
from reaching any precise end.
Yes, things are deprived of their former mandate
the Valley of Kings, neolithic Shang
    equally yielding to the epic of art,
beauty stripped of its power to function.

Temple, no temple, dissolve of our passions . . .

Temporally, spatially, the mind is a museum
Pretending to the objective but intangibly in flux.

Statuette of a cow
emerging from a papyrus swamp,
  only its head visible.

The three nude dancers glimpsed
through the center
of the perforated jade disk.

The cow's head, Hathor,
    no longer exclusively
a reified image:

The transparency of Hathor's neck
as she tilts through the hole,
its perforation seeming to widen
    to let her head pass

Episodes from a Possible *Nekyia*   111

until she's superimposed her form
    upon the moving figures
of the inexplicable dance.

Point on a planet
    into which
all the rest coils,
readers seeking entry
    to a soil that envelops them,
what seeds in whose remains
brewing themselves a continual nectar

With which to address the naked.

Sadly, we are not plants.

The cow's neck bent forward,
transparent/opaque.

The reader seeking entry.

A passage one reads again and again:

Crowded train depot, peoples dispersing,
delicate flesh yet concealed at the rush hour

Improvising within being's fullness,
though the direction never wavers.

Landscape

Hermes, scattered by storms, off his call,
Lies ruptured in our yard's shadows
Like a meteor that breaks apart

Imperceptibly blanketing the bare hills;
A mist in the air shaft
Hiding, without effort, the new Hermes.

Fire's ghost, a wisp of smoke
That scents the atmosphere as it once burnt the leaves,
The seen, the said, in vivio.

Fluorescent steam rollers
Boom in the streets like the roar of waves.

O you never alive

Being more essence than life,
More dust than letters

A terror calls, a sacred gasp
Still trapped in the cells of substitution

A bungled angel dying in a bottle
Like a wasp

Like a wolf howling in the tundra
This diaspora of fleshtones

Awaiting a frame to color —
Blonde clouds, raised to aberration —

Episodes from a Possible *Nekyia*

The seen, the said,
Names floating on a dark, wet transom.

Designed by
Samuel Retsov

᠅

Titles:Capelli
Text: Perpetua

᠅

acid-free paper

᠅

Printed by
McNaughton & Gunn